THE PACIFIC COAST AND ITS AGATES

The Pacific Coast [...] les, but few are as popu[...] fornia to Puget Sound, th[...] collect, and identify—once y[...]

While certain re[...] agate specimens than o[...] ey can survive the harsh wind and waves of the Pacific Ocean and can be transported far from their sources to more distant shores. From Mexico to Canada, agates are something beachcombers should always be on the lookout for. This map highlights just a few of the areas best known for agates, but remember that they can turn up almost anywhere along the coast.

AGATES AT A GLANCE

Concentric Banding: Agates' most defining trait is their concentric ring-like banded patterns, which repeat inward toward their center. Without this pattern, it isn't an agate.

Waxy Texture: Look for smooth stones with semi-shiny, "waxy" surfaces and textures.

Translucency: Agates are translucent and will "glow" in bright sunlight.

Very Hard: It's one of the hardest stones you'll find on the beach; a pocket knife won't scratch an agate.

Wide Range of Colors: Agates can have varying colors, sometimes within the same specimen. They are commonly white to gray, brown to reddish, yellow, bluish, or black.

Usually Small: The majority of the Pacific Coast's agates are quite small, generally under 2 inches, and most are much smaller. Pea-sized specimens are most common.

Map labels: San Juan Islands, Puget Sound, Olympic Peninsula, Seattle, Olympia, Astoria, Washington, Columbia River, Portland, Newport, Oregon, Coos Bay, Eureka, California, San Francisco, Pacific Ocean, Santa Barbara, Los Angeles

The Pacific Coast's agates can be found all along the western shores of Washington, Oregon, and California. On this map, the red highlights the coast and the yellow boxes highlight some of the historically most lucrative agate areas.

WHAT ARE AGATES?

Agates are the concentrically banded variety of **chalcedony** (pronounced "kal-SED-oh-nee"), which is itself a microcrystalline variety of quartz. **Quartz,** the single most common mineral on Earth, is composed of **silica,** or silicon dioxide, which is very hard, brittle, and resistant to weathering; it is found as a constituent of many types of rocks. While quartz ideally develops coarse, pointed, six-sided crystals, it can form under such a wide range of conditions that microcrystalline varieties, which appear as solid masses with crystal structures only visible under a microscope, are very abundant. These include chert, jasper, and chalcedony.

Chalcedony, which is translucent and often colorful due to impurities of other minerals, particularly iron compounds, does not usually exhibit banding; how it develops the onion-like layering seen in agates is still debated. There are numerous theories, but none have been conclusively proven. In fact, so many variations in agate structures exist around the world that there likely isn't just one correct theory of formation, but several.

What we do know, though, is that agates form within cavities in basalt, rhyolite, and other volcanic rocks. As the lava that formed these rocks cooled and hardened, gases were trapped as bubbles (called **vesicles**) within the molten rock that later became the pocket where silica could collect. As heated water from within the Earth inundated the new rock, it deposited silica and other minerals in the cavities, resulting in the growth of agates, quartz, and much more.

Common beach-worn examples, all measuring under 1/2 inch

This rough piece of basalt shows some empty vesicles as well as others filled with quartz and other minerals.

Common beach-worn basalt (left) and rhyolite (right)

AGATE STRUCTURE, SETTINGS, AND COLOR

The bands or layers in agates are not linear or flat; they are three-dimensional structures, and only when an agate is broken or cut can we see the bullseye-like cross section of the layers. What this means is that each layer or band is actually a shell that contains all the smaller shells within it. Think of agates like onions: they have numerous layers that repeat inward toward their center. And their layers tend to alternate in structure: dense, white and/or colored, less translucent chalcedony followed by coarser, more translucent and less colorful quartz grains. This is best appreciated in cut-and-polished specimens under a microscope, and this pattern indicates a complex means of formation.

Hot groundwater often deposits minerals in rock cavities, but not usually in such highly organized layers. It is thought that this occurs with chalcedony due to some unique properties of silica. Microcrystalline chalcedony requires more silica to form than regular quartz does; through a complex process of silica depletion and replenishment in groundwater, it has been convincingly proposed that a naturally repeating process deposited the layers two or three at a time, gradually creating the layered structure from the outside-in. The entire process is very complex, and there are several books devoted to the topic. But remember: while many theories are touted as "correct," agates have yet to be produced in a lab.

Most agates formed as a structure called an **amygdule,** which literally means "almond" in Latin, due to the generally rounded, tapering nature and almond-like shape of the gas cavities they formed within. Agates still preserved in host rock are often this shape. Specimens found loose on the beach are usually more irregular, largely due to weathering. Some agates can also form within cracks or fissures in rocks. These **vein** agates typically lack any rounded shapes unless highly weathered.

As hot, mineral-rich groundwater rises into the hollow vesicles of volcanic rocks, it can deposit chalcedony within the cavity, forming banding from outside-in.

HOW TO IDENTIFY AN AGATE

While it's not exactly clear how agates formed, there is no question about
the traits that define them. Appearance, hardness, and texture are all
taken into account—as well as their trademark banding, of course.

HARDNESS, TEXTURE, AND LUSTER

As with any form of quartz, agates are very hard.
In fact, quartz and all of its varieties are likely
going to be the hardest minerals you'll find
along the coast, requiring hardened steel
to scratch; a common pocket knife won't
leave a mark on an agate. This high
hardness makes agates very weather
resistant; wind and waves effectively
polishing specimens to a smooth, wax-like
sheen. Their waxy luster and texture are also identifying traits in beach-worn specimens. When not so worn down, the outer
surfaces of "fresh" agates often have small circular depressions (pits),
which developed when the agates were still within their host rock.

COLOR AND TRANSLUCENCY

Color and patterns are rarely good identifiers when it
comes to minerals, but with agates they are helpful.
Very pure agates are white to pale gray, often with
little contrast to make the banding visible, but
most have impurities that color their layers. Iron
compounds are the most abundant colorant, making
brown, red, orange, yellow, or green hues. In combi-
nation with chalcedony's translucency, which can
make agates appear to "glow" on sunlit beaches,
these wide variations give agates a distinctive and
attractive appearance.

FRACTURE

All forms of quartz, including agates,
exhibit conchoidal fracturing. This means
that when struck or broken, the shape
of the crack or break will be circular,
often appearing in crescent or ring-like
markings. And when freshly broken,
agates can have razor-sharp edges,
which may aid identification. In fact,
prehistoric peoples once made tools out
of chalcedony, chert, and even agate.

CONCENTRIC BANDING AND INCLUSIONS

The most important identifying trait of agates is, of course, their banding. There are lots of stones you'll find on the beach that may initially appear to have agate-like layers, but if they don't have the hardness, texture, and luster described on the previous page, *in addition* to a concentric banded pattern, then they aren't agates. The concentric banding is key; all the bands share a common center, and the largest, outermost band contains all the increasingly smaller interior bands within it. Agates are one of very few materials you'll find that exhibit this trait; most non-agate look-alikes will not have concentric bands. Not all agates will have a perfectly symmetrical pattern, but the concentric organization will still be readily apparent.

There do exist some agates with flat, parallel banding. These are commonly called **water-level** or water-line agates, and their formation was clearly different from that of typical agates. Many other rocks and minerals can exhibit parallel layering, but water-level agates are still easy to identify when considering all of the other agate-specific identifying traits outlined above.

Lastly, agates were rarely the only mineral that formed within their host rock's cavities. They usually shared the space with countless other materials, many of which can be found incorporated within agates. These include tree-like or needle-shaped growths of other minerals, which can interrupt and disturb the agate banding and provide an additional source of interest for collectors. These are called **inclusions,** and several prominent varieties with inclusions can be found along the Pacific Coast.

You may also find small agates with perfectly round "eyes" looking back at you. These are called agate eyes, and they formed when tiny hemispherical chalcedony growths— something all agates have but that are normally too small to see—have grown large. Though fairly rare and typically very small, these can be found on the Pacific Coast.

A quintessential example of a fortification agate, with an unusually symmetrical pattern

FORTIFICATION AGATES

Agates can take on a wide array of appearances and patterns, but the classic, concentric, band-within-a-band structure most associated with them is known as a fortification pattern, named for its similarity to a fort or castle's walls when viewed from above. These are the "truest" agates, and they formed under ideal conditions that allowed their banding to properly develop. As such, they also tend to be the most sought-after variety of agates, especially when finds have colorful and highly contrasting banding.

Fortification agates have ring-like bands by definition, but not all specimens will show a complete pattern. This is usually a result of a less-than-symmetrical pattern, but it can also simply be a result of weathering. Much of the Pacific Coast saw some glacial activity in the past ice ages, and the immense sheets of ice broke and wore down even the toughest rocks and minerals, including agates. Today, most agates found on beaches are not whole, but merely pieces of larger ones. As such, fortification patterns are often incomplete or obscured.

Fortification agates also frequently have a center cavity, called a **geode;** these resulted when agates didn't form completely. Similarly, they can also have a center filled with larger, coarser quartz crystals, thought to be a result of there not being enough available silica during formation to develop chalcedony, which requires more silica than typical quartz.

COLOR: Varies greatly; usually gray to brown, yellow, orange, or red

STRUCTURE: Ring-like bands that get smaller as they near the center of the agate, sometimes with a quartz-filled or hollow center

RARITY: Fortification agates are the most common variety.

WHERE TO LOOK: You'll find fortification agates virtually anywhere along the Pacific Coast; Oregon's coast is particularly lucrative.

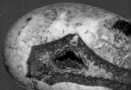

This gray-blue fortification agate has a hollow center; it is a geode.

The extremely fine water-level banding in this specimen turns into faint fortification banding near the top of the stone.

WATER-LEVEL AGATES

Water-level agates go by many names—onyx, water-line agates, gravitationally banded agates, or Uruguay-type agates (to get scientific)—but what is most clear is their dramatically different structure. They feature flat, parallel layers of microcrystalline quartz that could only have resulted from gravity causing silica to settle. This is thought to have occurred when more "watery" silica solutions pooled inside the cavity, as opposed to fortification banding, which is thought to have developed from a thick silica gel that was able to cling to the walls of the cavity. What makes water-level agates even more unusual is how many specimens will have a portion of parallel banding at the bottom with classic fortification banding above. This signifies a change in chemistry during formation and offers insight into how all agates formed.

Their horizontal layers show unique variations in structure as well; some layers are far more opaque than others and may change color along their length. It's not clear what causes such eccentricities. Water-level agates are not rare but are certainly scarcer than fortification agates.

This well-worn pebble is a fragment of a water-level agate, with several parallel bands visible.

COLOR: Varies greatly; usually gray to brown, yellow, orange, or red

STRUCTURE: Flat, horizontal, and parallel layers; sometimes these layers are only at the bottom of the specimen with fortification banding above.

RARITY: Somewhat common; water-level agates are not quite as abundant as fortification agates but are still frequently encountered.

WHERE TO LOOK: You'll potentially find water-level agates all along the Pacific Coast, but they are perhaps more common in Oregon, particularly around Newport.

It's easy to imagine the narrow pattern continuing from the right edge of this well-worn specimen.

VEIN AGATES

While most agates formed within vesicles, or the gas bubbles trapped within cooled volcanic rocks, resulting in rounded, nodular shapes, some did not. A few grew within cracks or fissures in rocks; they developed much in the same way as typical agates, but with elongated patterns that followed the contours of the broken rock cavity. These are called vein agates, also known as seam agates or fracture-filling agates. Most agates are believed to have formed shortly after the hardening of their host rock but while the surrounding area was still very hot. As heated groundwater brought silica into vesicles, it also brought it to the cracks that formed as the cooling rock contracted or was shifted by seismic activity.

Vein agates are distinguished from typical agates by their often flat, broad shapes and elongated, narrow banded patterns. When weathered and worn on the beach, however, they can begin to appear like any other agate as they break up. Look for agates whose patterns are narrow and symmetrical in their shortest direction, and look for any indication that the bands may have once been longer than the current boundaries of the specimen.

Note how the narrow banded pattern is virtually symmetrical.

COLOR: Varies greatly; usually gray to brown, yellow, orange, or red

STRUCTURE: Narrow banded patterns that are symmetrical in their shortest direction

RARITY: Fairly rare, if only because small weathered fragments appear like any other agate

WHERE TO LOOK: Vein agates are somewhat uncommon, but try searching near volcanic outcroppings; look along Oregon's coast into northern California, and in southern California north of Los Angeles.

INCLUSIONS

As agates formed, they frequently had to compete for space with other developing minerals. The other minerals were often incorporated into the resulting agate, where they are present today as inclusions that can interrupt or disturb the agate banding.

SAGENITE

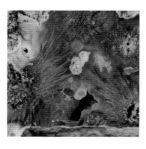

Sagenitic agates, or simply sagenites, are agates that contain needle-like mineral formations, often arranged in radial or circular groups. These are the result of other minerals, namely zeolites or goethite, that were incorporated into the agate. Later, these minerals were usually replaced by silica but retain the original mineral's shape. These are scarce along the Pacific Coast, but are most common in central to southern California, particularly near Nipomo.

MOSS AGATES

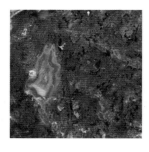

Certain iron compounds can chemically react with silica; within developing agates, these reactions create seemingly organic tangles and threads of color. Called moss agates for their mossy appearance, these are a popular and common type of inclusion more common in agates from more inland areas, but they can be found on beaches as well and may be encountered anywhere along the Pacific Coast. Sometimes the mossy inclusions are so opaque they're easy to confuse with jaspers.

IMPRESSIONS

Not all minerals that formed alongside an agate are still present. Certain soft minerals, like calcite, may have impressed themselves into a developing agate's banding but have since dissolved, leaving peculiar, angular holes behind. You'll see these often; the cavities appear smoother and more angular than a typical crack or break.

COLOR VARIETIES

Agates are popular not only for their banding, but also for the wide array of colors they can exhibit. But those colors aren't inherent to agates; they are caused by impurities within the chalcedony layers. Particularly pure agates are colorless to white or gray, but minerals bearing iron, aluminum, copper, manganese, and others can be present as microscopic grains within the bands. This can stain and tint the agates, producing the more collectible, colorful hues.

White agates are common and owe their faint coloration to a lack of impurities. Some may be so devoid of other minerals and cloudiness that they appear completely translucent in bright light.

Typical agates occur in shades of red, orange, brown, or yellow; these colors come from iron-bearing minerals. More exotic colors can be found along the coast, but in all cases, the most desirable specimens are those with lots of high-contrast banding, such as alternating bands of blue and white.

SURFACE COLORATIONS

While most agates will have largely the same coloration throughout the specimen, some exhibit colors that are only "skin deep." **Limonite,** an iron compound, can be deposited by groundwater onto the surface of agates. This opaque, yellow-brown substance is incorporated into the outermost layer of chalcedony and can usually be polished away. Similarly, some agates have white surface coloration called **bleaching;** in such finds, the color-causing impurities on outer surfaces have been removed, perhaps because of exposure to acidic groundwater (or other naturally occurring chemicals). Bleaching appears as white splotches and can add visual contrast to an agate's banding.

Opaque, peanut-butter-brown limonite coats the agate to the left, while the blue-black agate below gets its attractive contrast from opaque white surface bleaching.

Agate Varieties and Their Identification

CARNELIAN

The vivid red-orange hues of carnelian have long been popular along the Pacific. Its unmistakable coloration is caused by dense iron impurities staining very translucent chalcedony. Many carnelian agates have very low-contrast color variations, which can make their banding difficult to see, if any is present at all. Water-worn carnelian is common and can be found all along the coast, but Washington is particularly known for it; most samples will be small pea-sized pebbles.

PINK AND PURPLE AGATES

A rare pinkish agate from Newport, Oregon

Pink and purple agates are some of the most desirable and sought-after agate varieties on the Pacific Coast. They are also the rarest. When faintly colored, many agates may look pinkish in certain light, but the Newport, Oregon, area is home to truly pink agates, which are vividly colored in strawberry-lemonade hues. These are treasured by local collectors, as a good pink agate can be a one-in-one-thousand find. Similarly, some agates may appear to be purple; often, purplish coloration is an optical illusion caused by an interplay of translucent gray or bluish chalcedony and brown or reddish layers that are deeper within the specimen.

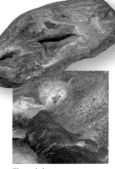

Though it may appear purplish, this agate is actually brown with an outer layer of blue-gray, which becomes apparent at other angles.

BLACK AND BLUE AGATES

Unusually high concentrations of impurities, likely of an aluminum- or manganese-rich composition, make some of the Pacific Coast's agates appear a very deep blue, sometimes so dark as to be nearly black. These desirable specimens often show prominent bleaching, giving their otherwise dark colors strong visual contrast. While fairly rare, they turn up with some frequency around Newport, Oregon.

Chalcedony can exhibit bulbous or rounded shapes that originate from its formation, as seen on the surface of this waxy pebble.

CHALCEDONY

Chalcedony is a common variety of quartz that is composed of tightly packed microcrystals that are shaped like tiny plates or fibers, and which usually grew in tiny stacks. This makes it translucent, especially in thin pieces. It has no regular outward shape and instead takes the shape of the cavity it formed within, such as gas bubbles or fissures in rocks. Coastal finds are often very rounded and smooth, usually with a waxy luster and texture, but they are also frequently found with highly fractured, pebbled surfaces. When freshly broken, chalcedony exhibits conchoidal (semicircular) breaks and fractures, usually with smooth surfaces and potentially sharp edges. As with many varieties of quartz, you may find chalcedony specimens still embedded in their host rock where their translucency and waxy texture contrasts with the surrounding rock, making it easier to spot. While chalcedony shares many physical traits with agates, and although all agates are composed of chalcedony, only concentrically banded (or water-level layered) chalcedony is considered agate.

This gray-brown chalcedony pebble shows the same waxy luster and conchoidal surface fractures as seen in agate, but without the concentric banding.

COLOR: Varies greatly; usually mottled gray to brown, yellow to orange, or reddish

OPACITY: Translucent; particularly thick or cloudy examples may only show translucency at their edges.

HARDNESS: Very hard; a pocket knife will not scratch it.

RARITY: Very common

WHERE TO LOOK: Chalcedony is common virtually anywhere along the coast. Any rock beach will yield countless examples.

Bright red jaspers are common and could be confused with carnelian if they weren't so opaque.

JASPER

This variety of quartz is composed of tightly packed but poorly organized quartz micro-grains, making it opaque. Usually defined as the more colorful variant of chert, jasper can exhibit a wide range of colors. It also has various layered, swirled, or mottled patterns that may resemble agate, but they differ because jasper's banding isn't always as finely delineated as that in agates. Any layering present in a jasper specimen usually appears coarser and "fuzzier," in addition to being opaque. Like chalcedony, it has no regular outward shape, instead appearing as masses that reflect the environment in which it formed. Because jasper can form in a variety of ways, including as very large masses in sedimentary rock formations, it can also appear on the shore in a variety of sizes. It is most often collected as weathered pebbles, which are usually smooth with a waxy texture and luster. Less worn samples are often much rougher and sharp-edged with a dull luster, looking more like a nondescript rock than a form of quartz.

The colorful layering in this jasper could be confused by some as an agate, but note how poorly defined the layers are.

COLOR: Varies greatly; usually gray to brown, yellow or red, often mottled or with irregular layering

OPACITY: Opaque; very thin fragments may be slightly translucent.

HARDNESS: Very hard; a pocket knife will not scratch it.

RARITY: Very common

WHERE TO LOOK: More abundant than chalcedony, you'll find jasper everywhere along the coast. The majority of the very hard, colorful pebbles you'll see on any cobble beach will be jasper.

Agate Look-alikes and Similar Materials

With a mottled, yet muted, coloration and solid opacity, there's no confusing this piece of chert with chalcedony.

CHERT

Chert is defined as a sedimentary rock and consists primarily of tightly packed, microscopic quartz grains, but it also contains minor amounts of other minerals. Chert formed on ancient seafloors when sediments settled—namely the silica skeletons of tiny organisms called diatoms—and it can infrequently exhibit nearly agate-like layers or banding. However, the bands are not nearly as well delineated as those in agates, instead often appearing slightly "blurred" or smudged. Usually, chert is mottled or solid and is colored in muted, dull tones. Like jasper, which is typically more colorful, chert is also opaque unless a specimen is very thin.

Chert usually has a rough, grainy, rock-like texture, though as with most quartz-based material, it can become very smooth and waxy when water-worn. It is very common and found on virtually any Pacific Coast beach, but it's easy to overlook because of its usually mundane appearance. With that said, nicely smoothed, layered specimens can be worth collecting.

Hard, dense, and dull-colored; here's a common example of greenish chert. While still a variety of quartz, it is easy to see the difference between chert and agate.

COLOR: Varies; usually gray to black, yellow to greenish, or tan to brown

OPACITY: Opaque

HARDNESS: Very hard; a pocket knife will not scratch it.

RARITY: Very common

WHERE TO LOOK: Found virtually everywhere, chert is one of the most abundant varieties of quartz. It is so weather-resistant that pebbles are nearly everywhere; on cobble beaches you'll easily walk over countless pieces without realizing it.

Quartzite is frequently nearly pink in color, but with a grainy texture that differs from chalcedony. Also note the whitish flaky areas characteristic of quartzite.

QUARTZITE

A metamorphic rock that began as sandstone, quartzite consists primarily of cemented grains of quartz. As such, it is quite hard and weather resistant, and is commonly found as rounded beach cobbles on virtually any of the Pacific Coast's shores. It is usually somewhat translucent but with a very grainy or sometimes flaky texture, even when weathered, which distinguishes it from chalcedony and agates. It can have layers of color that may resemble that of a water-level agate, but quartzite's layers are usually coarser and more poorly delineated than those in agates. More frequently, quartzite is solidly colored with no banding, resembling common quartz more than agate. Quartzite, however, is not as glassy as quartz when freshly broken. Samples with bolder coloration also tend to be far more opaque, as the color-causing impurities add to their overall opacity.

Though it does have horizontal banding, you wouldn't confuse this piece of quartzite for an agate due to its opacity, the poorly defined layers, and the fact that the layers aren't all parallel.

COLOR: Varies greatly; usually gray to brown, yellow, red, or black

OPACITY: Usually semi-translucent unless very thick or colorful, then opaque

HARDNESS: Very hard; a pocket knife may scratch it with some effort.

RARITY: Common

WHERE TO LOOK: Quartzite can be found in the cobbles of most coastal beaches, particularly closer to mountain ranges, such as the Olympic Mountains or those in southern California.

Most beach quartz will be found as rounded pebbles, like this particularly pure and white example. Others will show up with other minerals or rock fragments mixed in, as in the specimen on the left.

QUARTZ

The most common single mineral in the Earth's crust and the most abundant form of silica, quartz is found as a constituent of most rocks. Its most ideal form is as transparent six-sided crystals, but it is more frequently encountered as grains, irregular masses, or in its microcrystalline forms, such as chert and jasper. Most beach finds are angular, sharp-edged, glassy masses when fresh, or rounded pebbles resembling frosted glass. If you're lucky enough to find quartz crystals on the shore, they will most often be found as tiny "glittery" points within cavities in rocks where they have been more protected from the elements. Though they both share many traits, quartz is unlikely to be confused with agate, but masses may easily be confused with quartzite. Quartz, however, lacks the grainy, flaky texture of quartzite; quartz will also break in smoother, glassier sections, as opposed to quartzite's irregular, grainy breaks.

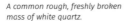

A common rough, freshly broken mass of white quartz.

COLOR: Most commonly colorless to white or gray; frequently stained yellow to brown or reddish, occasionally green

OPACITY: Transparent to translucent

HARDNESS: Very hard; a pocket knife will not scratch it.

RARITY: Very common

WHERE TO LOOK: Quartz is widely available all along the coast. Its typically white, translucent coloration makes it easy to spot.

Agate Look-alikes and Similar Materials

Jasper, such as this reddish piece, frequently has quartz veining within old cracks.

MINERAL VEINS

When rocks and minerals crack and break as a result of weathering or from forces within the Earth, such as earthquakes or volcanic eruptions, the resultant fractures can later fill with quartz, calcite, or other minerals. These minerals, introduced later by mineral-bearing groundwater, can "heal" the stones, solidifying their fragments while also giving them a striped appearance. Called veins, most of these formations don't look much like agates, but some newcomers may mistake their lines for agate banding at first. Finds with mineral veins are usually very common once you start looking for them, and they rarely have any agate-like qualities, but they are neat finds and can be collectible in their own right.

In the San Juan Islands, entire beaches consist largely of beautiful veined stones. The San Juans are a National Monument, though, so collecting there is illegal.

COLOR: Varies; usually white to gray or yellowish veins within rocks of varying darker color

OPACITY: Usually opaque

HARDNESS: Varies depending on the vein mineral; quartz and calcite are both common vein minerals—calcite is easily scratched by a pocket knife, but quartz is not.

RARITY: Common

WHERE TO LOOK: Rocks containing mineral veins are abundant all along the coast, particularly in the more volcanically active regions; the San Juan Islands are especially rich with veined stones.

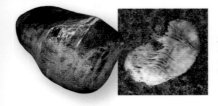

This piece of petrified wood as it was found on a sandy beach. Note the elongated woodgrain pattern.

PETRIFIED WOOD

An unusual and exciting find along the Pacific Coast is petrified (fossilized) wood. More often associated with deserts than with beaches, this ancient wood-turned-rock is usually composed of a variety of quartz, particularly jasper. This makes it resistant to weathering, where it becomes rounded and smoothed in the waves.

Petrified wood formed when ancient wood was buried instead of rotting; it was then inundated by mineral-rich water. The minerals in the water replaced the wood material but preserved its appearance and structure. Petrified wood often looks like any other rounded beach cobble, but it is identified by its finely layered wood-grain structure preserved in the rock. It can also appear somewhat porous, which also reflects its organic origins, and very fine specimens of large enough size can even exhibit tree-growth rings. However, many beach specimens lack clear details, so collectors can be left guessing. If you don't have distinctive evidence, you probably haven't found petrified wood.

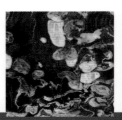

Teredo wood is a particular variety of petrified wood that contains countless tunnels and holes made by an ancient mollusk. Though rare, it turns up on Oregon's beaches.

COLOR: Varies; usually white to gray, tan, brown, or nearly black

OPACITY: Opaque

HARDNESS: Varies, but usually quite hard; may be scratched with a pocket knife with effort.

RARITY: Scarce

WHERE TO LOOK: Your best chance will be along central Oregon's coasts, particularly from Cannon Beach south to Bandon and beyond. The Neskowin area is home to a submerged petrified "forest" that reveals itself at low tide, but collecting there is not allowed.

OTHER FOSSILS

It should come as no surprise that the Pacific Coast is home to fossils of ancient marine life, particularly shellfish. From snails to scallops, the coast's sandstone, shale, and limestone—all rocks of aquatic origin—can contain the hard, mineralized remains of ancient sea animals. Shells are often visible in rocks as small curved structures; carefully breaking the rock can reveal more of the shell within.

Most Pacific Coast fossil finds will merely be indications of organic matter. In the sample above, fragments of shells can be seen edge-on; careful breaking of the sandstone could reveal more of the shells' structures, but it will more likely cause the delicate features to crumble.

Carefully splitting the sandstone concretion to the right revealed a full scallop shell fossil. Before breaking open the stone, only a tiny edge was visible, as in the upper photo.

Snail shells in chert, as seen just below, are not rare, but they are often small and easily overlooked, especially when the distinctive coil shape hasn't been fully exposed or is incomplete.

COLOR: Varies; usually white to tan or brown

OPACITY: Opaque

HARDNESS: Usually fairly soft, easily scratched with a pocket knife unless the fossil is composed of chert or jasper

RARITY: Scarce

WHERE TO LOOK: Small fossils may be found sparingly all along the coast, but central Oregon's coast is particularly known for fossil-bearing sandstone.

Most beach finds of jade resemble this: dark green with smooth, waxy luster and surfaces all around, often with veins or splotches of brown or tan coloration.

JADE

A long-favored collectible, jade is one of the rarer treasures available to Pacific beachcombers. Famed for its color and how easy it is to carve and shape, the name "jade" actually refers to two separate minerals—jadeite and nephrite (nephrite is actually the name for the gem variety of the mineral actinolite)—which share a similar appearance. Both develop as masses of semi-translucent material with mottled coloration in shades of light to dark green, often with mottled yellows, tans, browns, and black spotting. Jade is usually found in water-worn pebbles, which have a waxy or greasy luster; particularly translucent pieces could be confused with green chalcedony or other quartz material. Jade is rarer than quartz-based materials, though, and it is slightly softer.

This polished specimen shows some of the finer details within typical beach jade, including black mineral spots.

COLOR: Light to dark green, often mottled with black spots; sometimes brownish

OPACITY: Semi-translucent; thick masses are opaque.

HARDNESS: Fairly hard; may be scratched with a pocket knife with some effort, but slightly softer than quartz or chalcedony

RARITY: Rare

WHERE TO LOOK: Jade can rarely be found all along the coast, but you'll perhaps have the best luck on northern California's coasts and into southern Oregon.

This specimen of calcite, freshly broken from seaside rock, shows angular and brightly reflective planes and facets, as opposed to the dull, chalky, rounded calcite veins in the rock shown on the left.

CALCITE

One of the world's most common minerals, calcite is found in a wide range of geological environments and is quite common on beaches in various forms. It frequently develops as white masses or veins within other rocks, but it is so soft that it easily weathers and wears away on active beaches. On the coast, you'll most frequently encounter calcite as soft bands within rocks, sometimes with a chalky or grainy texture as it wears down. Its low hardness is a key identifying trait, as is the specific way it breaks: when struck, it breaks into step-like groups of rhombohedrons, which is a shape like a skewed or "leaning" cube. It is also possible that you could find calcite as small crystals within cavities in rock, particularly sedimentary rocks. When crystallized, it can take many forms, but it most frequently occurs as small six-sided, steeply angled points, or rhombohedrons.

It is easily distinguished from quartz by its low hardness alone, but when in doubt, put a small piece of calcite into vinegar. Calcite will bubble and fizz as it dissolves, but quartz will not react.

These calcite crystals show their trademark rhombohedral shape, resembling a "leaning" cube. When freshly broken, calcite will break into shapes like this.

COLOR: Typically white, but often gray to brown

OPACITY: Translucent

HARDNESS: Soft, easily scratched with a pocket knife

RARITY: Common

WHERE TO LOOK: Calcite can be found all along the Pacific Coast, but you'll have better luck along adjoining river banks or where more recent erosion has occurred.

The strange appearance of this sandstone cliff is the result of dozens of concretions that have weathered and fallen from their host rock.

CONCRETIONS

Concretions are peculiar, unusually round rocks. Unlike most beach rocks, they were not shaped by weathering but instead formed that way. The often spherical or globular shapes originally formed inside another body of rock—usually sandstone or shale—as a result of chemical reactions that caused minerals to nucleate, or collect, around a central point (often a small fossil or other organic fragment). The often dark-colored, ball-like concretions are frequently harder than their host and are freed by weathering. They can leave behind a peculiar network of holes in their host rock, too, sometimes not unlike a honeycomb. Most concretions are found in or near their host rock, where they are especially conspicuous. On a typical beach, however, their round shapes can perfectly blend with the rest of the cobbles. Identifying them can be difficult, but generally they are more spherical than the average beach rock, often with rougher surfaces that indicate that they formed with that shape instead of being rounded by wave action. When in doubt, though, you may have to ask a professional.

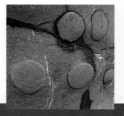

These tightly embedded concretions have almost the same coloration as their host rock.

COLOR: Brown to gray

OPACITY: Opaque

HARDNESS: Varies; usually soft and can be scratched with a pocket knife

RARITY: Scarce

WHERE TO LOOK: Concretions are usually found near their source; any beachside cliffs, hills, or riverbanks are good places to start, particularly in northern California or along Puget Sound.

Whole fishing net floats are very rare but popular finds. This blue-green example is dulled by weathering.

BEACH GLASS

Despite the natural wonders found all along the Pacific Coast, beach glass remains a perennial favorite among some collectors. Beginning as common man-made objects—glass bottles, fishing net floats, electrical insulators, etc.—the waves and rocks can break up the litter to produce shards that are rounded and smoothed in the same way as any rock. The resultant pebbles of translucent glass show up in a variety of colors with frosted surfaces. These can look very similar to quartz, though on a fresh break it should be easy to observe that the glass has no irregularities in structure or color within. In addition, glass tends to have a more uniform thickness, and it should be scarcer than quartz pebbles on most beaches. Occasionally, whole glass objects can appear on shore, such as glass fishing net floats. These look like orbs of clear or green glass, many of which could have been at sea for decades and originated mostly from Japanese or southeast Asian fishermen, who used them to keep their nets afloat.

The beach at MacKerricher State Park is dense with glass fragments that seem to outnumber the rocks.

COLOR: Varies; commonly colorless, green, blue, or brown; rarely red

OPACITY: Transparent to translucent

HARDNESS: Hard, not easily scratched with a pocket knife

RARITY: Very common as fragments; whole fishing floats are very rare.

WHERE TO LOOK: Can be found virtually anywhere, including areas seemingly untouched by people, due to wave action washing items ashore. Glass Beach at MacKerricher State Park in California is a beach seemingly made entirely of tumbled beach glass derived from decades of the nearby town dumping garbage into the ocean.

FINAL NOTES

This guide is meant to help new collectors identify agates and agate-like materials, along with some additional popular finds. For help identifying more unusual finds, consult a guide with a more complete selection of rocks and minerals. But before you do that, be sure that wishful thinking isn't clouding your identification process. As a general rule, never assume that you've found something rare or valuable while casually walking the beach; rare materials almost always take considerable effort to find. The following is a list of commonly confused materials:

Gold—Finding gold on the beach is very unlikely. Golden or brassy colored finds are usually pyrite, chalcopyrite, or mica; all are far more common.

Meteorites—Virtually every black to brown metallic mass that sticks to a magnet is the mineral magnetite, not a meteorite fallen from space. Magnetite is very common on Pacific Coast beaches.

Diamonds—Finding a diamond on the beach is not unheard of but is extremely unlikely. Most beach "diamonds" are simply lustrous, clear quartz fragments. If you suspect a diamond, identification will be easy: no other mineral or tool will scratch a diamond, including silicon carbide (a component of certain drill bits), which easily mars quartz.

BEACHCOMBING SAFETY

No matter where you are along the Pacific Coast, you must always be acutely aware of the tides. Some areas experience faster, stronger tides than others, and rising water can catch you by surprise, leaving you stranded or worse. Tide charts can help you plot when and where tidal movement occurs; you should familiarize yourself with these tools before setting out.

Seaside cliffs and hills may be beautiful, but they are often unstable, particularly after rain. Mudslides and cliff collapses are frequent along the coast, so stay off of these landforms and don't spend time below them.

PRIVATE PROPERTY AND PROTECTED AREAS

At all times, it is your responsibility to know where you are collecting. Trespassing on private property, collecting in protected park areas, and collecting more than the weight limit allowed in each state are all prohibited activities that will result in fines from authorities. Please respect private property lines and be mindful and careful of our natural spaces.

GLOSSARY

Silica—A natural chemical compound consisting of silicon and oxygen

Quartz—The hardened mineral form of silica; quartz is the most common mineral and has many different forms

Chalcedony—A form of quartz consisting of microscopic crystals arranged into fibers; chalcedony is the primary constituent of agates

Vesicle—A round cavity in volcanic rocks formed by trapped gas; the typical cavity in which agates form

Volcanic—Relating to rocks formed by the hardening of molten rock originating from deep within the Earth

Concentric—A pattern in which each layer or shape shares the same center

Agate—The concentrically banded form of chalcedony, usually formed within vesicles in volcanic rocks

Crystal—A solid body with a repeating atomic structure formed when an element or inorganic chemical compound solidifies; the hardened form of natural, inorganic chemicals

Band—An easily identified layer of differing color within a rock or mineral

Rock—A massive aggregate of mineral grains

Mineral—A naturally occurring inorganic chemical compound that solidifies with a definite and repeating internal crystal structure

RECOMMENDED READING

Bonewitz, Ronald Louis. *Smithsonian Rock and Gem*. New York: DK Publishing, 2005.

Chesteman, Charles W. *The Audubon Society Field Guide to North American Rocks and Minerals*. New York: Knopf, 1979.

Lynch, Dan R., and Bob Lynch. *The Wonder of North American Agates*. Cambridge: Adventure Publications, 2013.

Lynch, Dan R., and Bob Lynch. *Rocks & Minerals of California*. Cambridge: Adventure Publications, 2017.

Lynch, Dan R., and Bob Lynch. *Rocks & Minerals of the Pacific Coast*. Cambridge: Adventure Publications, 2018.

Lynch, Dan R., and Bob Lynch. *Rocks & Minerals of Washington and Oregon*. Cambridge: Adventure Publications, 2012.

Mottana, Annibale, et al. *Simon and Schuster's Guide to Rocks and Minerals*. New York: Simon and Schuster, 1978.

Pough, Frederick H. *Rocks and Minerals*. Boston: Houghton Mifflin, 1988.

Robinson, George W. *Minerals*. New York: Simon & Schuster, 1994.

Adventure Quick Guides

Beachcombing in California, Oregon, and Washington

Organized by rocks/minerals, then by appearance, for quick and easy identification

—SIMPLE AND CONVENIENT—

narrow your choices by group, and view just a few photos at a time

- Pocket-sized format—easier than laminated foldouts
- Professional photos showing key traits
- Tips for identifying rocks and minerals
- Six varieties of agates, as well as popular finds like Jasper, Quartz, and Jade

Celebrate agates with the beautiful book and playing cards!

NATURE / ROCKS & MINERALS / PACIFIC COAST
ISBN 978-1-59193-933-7   **$9.95**

5 0 9 9 5

9 781591 939337

Adventure PUBLICATIONS
an imprint of Adventure**KEEN**